SCHOLASTIC

News

Nonfiction Readers®

What Is the Story of Our Flag?

By Janice Behrens

Children's Press®
An Imprint of Scholastic Inc.
New York Toronto London Auckland Sydney
Mexico City New Delhi Hong Kong
Danbury, Connecticut

These content vocabulary word builders are for grades 1–2.

Subject Consultant: Eli J. Lesser, MA, Director of Education, National Constitution Center, Philadelphia, Pennsylvania

Reading Consultant: Cecilia Minden-Cupp, PhD, Early Literacy Consultant and Author, Chapel Hill, North Carolina

Photographs © 2009: Alamy Images: 23 bottom left (Bryan & Cherry Alexander Photography), 21 bottom left (Oote Boe Photography), 17 bottom right (Ian Dagnall), 2 (Daniel Dempster Photography), 21 top right (Image Farm Inc.), 17 top right (Gabe Palmer), 4 top, 12 (Joe Sohm/Visions of America, LLC), 20 left (Vstock); Courtesy of Bureau of Reclamation, Lower Colorado: 23 top left; Corbis Images: 13 top left (Owen Franken), 23 bottom right (Smithsonian Institution); JupiterImages/Thinkstock: 17 bottom left; Masterfile: 4 bottom right, 5 bottom right, 6 (Miles Ertman), 5 top left, 16 (Jon Feingersh); NASA: 17 top left; New York Public Library Picture Collection: 13 bottom left, 13 bottom right; NEWSCOM: back cover, 5 top right, 18 (Richard B. Levine), 11; PhotoEdit: 21 top left (Robert W. Ginn), 1, 15 (Michael Ventura); The Granger Collection, New York: 4 bottom left, 10 (Henry Mosler), 13 top right, 23 top right; The Image Works/Michael Siluk: 9; VEER: 19, 20 right (Blend Images Photography), 7 (Image Source Photography), cover (Stockbyte Photography). Maps by James McMahon

Series Design: Simonsays Design!
Art Direction, Production, and Digital Imaging: Scholastic Classroom Magazines

Library of Congress Cataloging-in-Publication Data
Behrens, Janice, 1972-
What is the story of our flag? / Janice Behrens.
    p. cm. – (Scholastic news nonfiction readers)
Includes bibliographical references and index.
ISBN 13: 978-0-531-21093-2 (lib. bdg.)   978-0-531-22430-4 (pbk.)
ISBN 10: 0-531-21093-6 (lib. bdg.)   0-531-22430-9 (pbk.)
1. Flags–United States–Juvenile literature. I. Title. II. Series.
CR113.B37 2009
929.9'20973–dc22   2008028623

©2009 Scholastic Inc.
All rights reserved. Published in 2009 by Children's Press, an imprint of Scholastic Inc.
Published simultaneously in Canada. Printed in the United States of America. 44

SCHOLASTIC, CHILDREN'S PRESS, and associated logos are trademarks and/or registered trademarks of Scholastic Inc.
1 2 3 4 5 6 7 8 9 10 R 18 17 16 15 14 13 12 11 10 09

CONTENTS

WORD HUNT

Look for these words as you read. They will be in **bold**.

field
(feeld)

seamstress
(**seem**-struhss)

stars
(starz)

flagpole
(**flag**-pohl)

parade
(puh-**rade**)

states
(states)

stripes
(stripes)

What Is the Story of Our Flag?

Our flag is red, white, and blue. It has **stars** and **stripes**. But did you know that the American flag has not always looked the same?

stars

stripes

The American flag is sometimes called the Stars and Stripes.

When our country was new, the leaders decided we needed a flag. Back then, there were only 13 **states**. The first flag had a star and a stripe for each state.

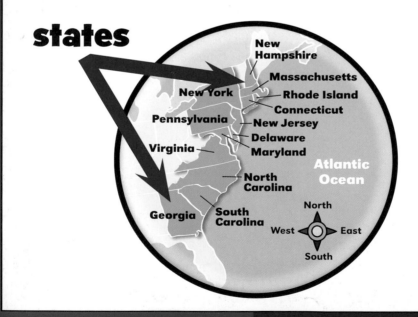

states

New Hampshire
Massachusetts
New York
Rhode Island
Connecticut
Pennsylvania
New Jersey
Delaware
Virginia
Maryland
Atlantic Ocean
North Carolina
Georgia
South Carolina

North
West ◉ East
South

The first flag had 13 stars and 13 stripes, like this one. Count them!

Who made the first flag?
No one knows for sure.
Some people think it was
a **seamstress** who lived in
Philadelphia. Her name was
Betsy Ross.

seamstress

This woman works at a museum called the Betsy Ross House. She can show you how the first flag was made.

Over the years, new states joined the country. Stars were added to the blue **field**. Sometimes the stars were in a circle. Other times they were in rows.

Sometimes stripes were added too.

field

1776

1795

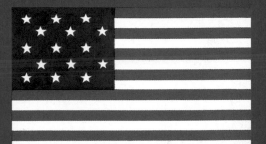

Can you count the stars and stripes on these old flags?

1803

1856

13

Our flag today has 50 stars. There is one for each state. It has 13 stripes, for the first 13 states. When people see the flag, they think of our country.

Where have you seen the Stars and Stripes?

Children in this school say the Pledge of Allegiance to the flag.

The flag flies in many places. It flies at ball games and post offices. There is a **flagpole** on top of the White House, where the President lives. Astronauts put the flag on the moon!

flagpole

Can you think of other places you see the flag?

You might see the flag in a **parade** on June 14. That is Flag Day, the birthday of the American flag. It is a day to be proud of the Stars and Stripes.

parade

HOW WE TREAT OUR FLAG

When we handle the American flag, we follow these rules. Following the rules is a way of showing respect for the flag, and for the country it stands for.

2 We never let the flag touch the ground.

1 We raise the flag quickly and lower it slowly.

3 We always fold the flag into the shape of a triangle. When the flag is completely folded, only the stars and the field of blue can be seen.

Do you know why the flag sometimes flies at half-mast?
The flag flies at half-mast, or raised only halfway up the flagpole, as a sign of respect when someone important dies.

YOUR NEW WORDS

field (feeld) a space on which something is drawn or placed

flagpole (**flag**-pohl) a tall pole for raising and flying a flag

parade (puh-**rade**) a line of people who march along as part of a celebration. A parade can have music, dancers, cars, and other vehicles.

seamstress (**seem**-struhss) a woman who sews for other people

stars (starz) a shape with five or more points

states (states) groups of people under one government. Today there are 50 states in the United States.

stripes (stripes) narrow bands of color

FOUR FAMOUS AMERICAN FLAGS

The biggest flag is called Superflag.

Explorers put a flag at the North Pole.

Explorers put a flag at the South Pole.

This old flag was made in 1813.

INDEX

FIND OUT MORE
Book:
Thomson, Sarah L. *Stars and Stripes: The Story of the American Flag.*
New York: HarperCollins, 2003.

Website:
www.theholidayspot.com/flagday/index.htm

MEET THE AUTHOR
Janice Behrens is a writer and Scholastic editor. She lives
with her husband and daughter in New York City.
She learned about folding the flag long, long ago when
she was a Girl Scout.